Essential Life Science

MICROORGANISMS

Louise and Richard Spilsbury

Heinemann
LIBRARY

Chicago, Illinois

Edited by Andrew Farrow and Diyan Leake
Designed by Victoria Allen
Original illustrations © Capstone Global
    Library Ltd 2014
Picture research by Ruth Blair
Production by Sophia Argyris
Originated by Capstone Global Library Ltd
Printed in China by CTPS

17 16 15 14 13
10 9 8 7 6 5 4 3 2

Library of Congress Cataloging-in-Publication Data
Spilsbury, Louise.
  Microorganisms / Louise and Richard Spilsbury.
    p. cm.—(Essential life science)
  Summary: "Our world is filled with living things
too small to see. Some of these microorganisms are
harmful, and some are helpful. This book explores the
amazing diversity of microorganisms and looks at how
we depend on them."—Provided by publisher.
  Includes bibliographical references and index.
  ISBN 978-1-4329-7811-2 (hb)—ISBN 978-1-4329-
7842-6 (pb) 1. Microorganisms—Juvenile literature. 2.
Microbiology—Juvenile literature. I. Spilsbury, Richard,
1963- II. Title. III. Series: Essential life science.
  QR57.S66 2014
  579—dc23   2012051333

Acknowledgments
We would like to thank the following for
permission to reproduce photographs: Alamy
pp. 11 (© Aquascopic), 18 (© Richard Griffin), 26
(© SuperStock), 38 (© Doug Perrine); Capstone
Publishers (© Karon Dubke) pp. 12, 13, 24, 25, 36,
37, 42; Corbis pp. 6 (© Reg Morrison/Auscape/
Minden Pictures), 15 (© 3d4Medical.com), 16
(© Martin Ruetschi/Keystone), 30 (© doable/
amanaimages), 31 (© John Rensten); Getty Images
pp. 4 (G. Wanner), 7 (Dr. Fred Hossler), 9 (CNRI/
Science Photo Library), 17 (Camilla Watson), 21
(Kallista Images), 28 (Peter Dazeley), 29 (Digital
Vision), 35 (Blackpool College /Oxford Scientific),
40 (Visuals Unlimited, Inc./Gregory Basco), 41 (Don
Johnston); Shutterstock pp. 14 (© Monkey Business
Images), 17 (© Jultud), 19 (© Elenamiv), 23 (© Rido),
32 (© bofotolux), 33 (© carroteater), 34 (© BMJ), 39
(© Henrik Larsson); Superstock pp. 10 (Johner), 43
(Blend Images).

Cover photograph of anthrax bacteria reproduced
with permission of Getty Images (MedicalRF.com).

Every effort has been made to contact copyright
holders of material reproduced in this book. Any
omissions will be rectified in subsequent printings
if notice is given to the publisher.

Contents

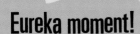

Eureka moment!

Learn about important discoveries that have brought about further knowledge and understanding.

 DID YOU KNOW?

Discover fascinating facts about microorganisms.

WHAT'S NEXT?

Read about the latest research and advances in essential science.

Some words are shown in bold, **like this**. You can find out what they mean by looking in the glossary.

What Are Microorganisms?

Microorganisms are tiny living things that are too small for us to see with just our eyes. The word *microorganism* is short for *microscopic organism*, which means they are living things we can only see with a **microscope.**

There are microorganisms everywhere: in the air, soil, and water, on food, and on and in our bodies. In this book, we are going to look at the four main types of microorganism: bacteria, viruses, fungi, and protists.

A single bacteria is called a bacterium. Millions of bacteria can fit on the point of a single pin! There are more bacteria than any other type of living thing found on the planet.

Eureka moment!

When Dutch scientist Antonie van Leeuwenhoek was looking at scrapings from his teeth through a very simple microscope in 1674, he became the first person to observe microorganisms.

Harmless or helpful?

Microorganisms are also known as **microbes**. Over 95 percent of microbes are harmless, and many of them are actually useful or even very good for us. The remaining 5 percent can cause illnesses such as colds, flu, and stomachaches. We often call microbes that harm us germs or bugs, but their scientific name is **pathogens**. Microbes can enter our bodies in different ways, such as from the air, touch, water, food, and animals.

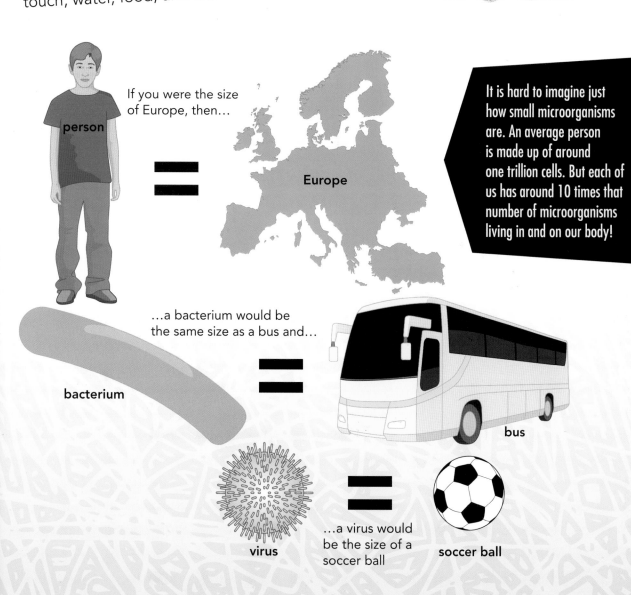

person

If you were the size of Europe, then…

Europe

It is hard to imagine just how small microorganisms are. An average person is made up of around one trillion cells. But each of us has around 10 times that number of microorganisms living in and on our body!

…a bacterium would be the same size as a bus and…

bacterium

bus

virus

…a virus would be the size of a soccer ball

soccer ball

What Are Bacteria Like?

Many living things are made up of millions of **cells**, but bacteria consist of only one cell. They are **unicellular**. Cells are the smallest units of living matter, often called the building blocks of all living things. Some bacteria exist as single cells all the time; other bacteria cluster together in pairs, chains, or other groupings. Bacteria were among the first forms of life on Earth billions of years ago. They were involved in creating the **atmosphere** that we breathe today.

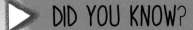

DID YOU KNOW?

Most bacteria are microscopic. However, the largest one, whose scientific name is *Thiomargarite namibiensis*, is about as big as the period at the end of this sentence.

Stromatolites are rock-like structures built by a type of bacteria called cyanobacteria. These structures are about 3,000 years old, but they are similar to those living on Earth 3.5 billion years ago!

There are thousands of different types of bacteria, but most of them are shaped like balls, rods, or spirals. Some bacteria also have parts called **flagella** that look like little tails. They use flagella to push themselves through liquids. Some bacteria move around in water, in the air, or on passing animals. Some release a thin layer of slime to slither over, the way slugs do. Other bacteria always stay in roughly the same spot.

Eureka moment!

Scientists have brought a 500-million-year-old bacterium back to life by growing it inside modern bacteria. They hope to find out whether the bacterium will **evolve** the same way it did in the past or whether it will develop into a new, different microbe.

flagella

Bacteria spin their flagella around and around like a small boat's outboard motor to swim from place to place.

How do bacteria work?

Bacteria come in different shapes, but each cell has basically the same structure. Most have a thick outer covering called the **cell wall** that gives the cell its shape, like the scaffolding around a building. Just inside the cell wall is the cell membrane. This works like a gate to control what substances go in and out of the cell. Many bacteria also have pili along their surface. Pili are like little hairs that help bacteria cling to surfaces. Cytoplasm is the liquid that fills the cell.

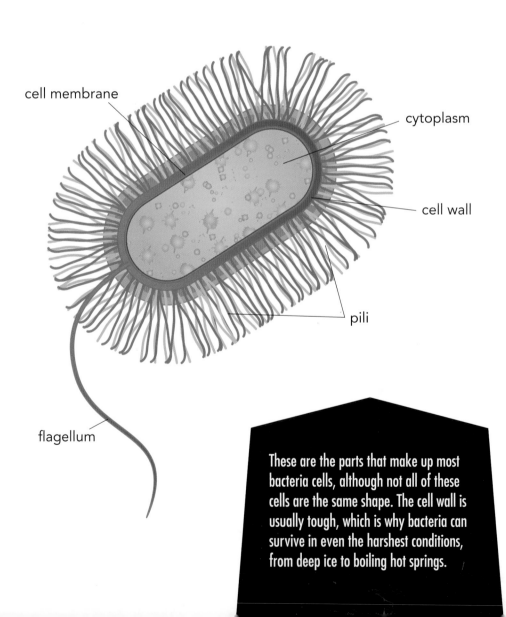

cell membrane

cytoplasm

cell wall

pili

flagellum

These are the parts that make up most bacteria cells, although not all of these cells are the same shape. The cell wall is usually tough, which is why bacteria can survive in even the harshest conditions, from deep ice to boiling hot springs.

Bacteria can live almost anywhere, but they generally grow faster in warm, moist conditions—including inside the human body. Bacteria grow in number, not in size. They multiply by splitting in two. Then those two cells each split in two, and so on. Each cell is identical to the original cell. This process is called binary fission. It is why bacteria can multiply amazingly fast. Their **reproduction** slows down when they begin to run out of space, food, and other things they need to stay alive.

DID YOU KNOW?

When it is cold, bacteria become **inactive**. They can rest for a very long time, until it warms up and they start to reproduce again. Many bacteria start to die when the temperature goes above 140 degrees Fahrenheit (60 degrees Celsius).

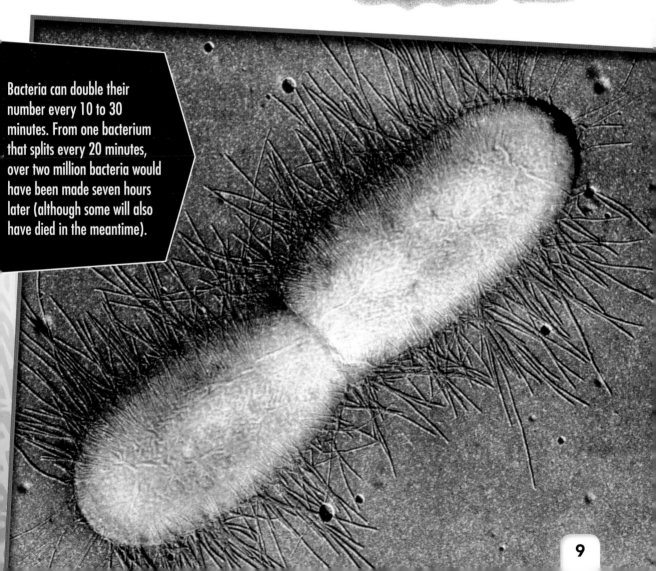

Bacteria can double their number every 10 to 30 minutes. From one bacterium that splits every 20 minutes, over two million bacteria would have been made seven hours later (although some will also have died in the meantime).

What do bacteria eat?

Some bacteria make their own food by **photosynthesis**, just like plants. Cyanobacteria use energy from sunlight to mix **carbon dioxide** (a gas in the air) with water to make sugars. Other bacteria absorb food from the material they live on or in. Most bacteria feed on **organic** matter (substances that were or are alive), but some types eat different things, including body sweat!

Sweat doesn't usually smell, but we need to wash it off regularly. This is because bacteria that live on our skin will feed on sweat, releasing chemicals that can smell.

▶ DID YOU KNOW?

When bacteria make food by photosynthesis, they release **oxygen** into the atmosphere. Cyanobacteria were the only life-forms on Earth for 2 billion years. They introduced the oxygen into the air that living things (including humans) depend on!

When bacteria feed on organic matter, they **decompose** it, or break it down. If you leave food out in the open, it begins to rot. That is because bacteria eat the food and then use that energy to make more bacteria. Some bacteria eat dead and decaying matter, such as waste. Some bacteria damage underground cables by eating through plastic covering the wires, and some grow as a thin layer on the surface of metal, causing the metal to decay and fall apart.

WHAT'S NEXT?

Some scientists think that in the future, we might use bacteria to convert bathroom waste solids and vegetable waste into methane gas that could be used to power our stoves. Methane digesters are already used in some places, but they could be used to directly recycle home waste.

Metal-munching bacteria are helping to rot away sunken ships at the bottom of the ocean.

Try this!

The coating you feel on your teeth when they need brushing is a layer of bacteria called plaque. Plaque makes harsh substances called **acids** that cause cavities (holes) in teeth.

Prediction

Coating eggshell with a layer of toothpaste should protect it from an acid such as vinegar.

What you need

- Vinegar (be careful with this and keep it away from your eyes)
- Clear nail polish
- A fresh egg (still in its shell)
- A wide-brimmed glass
- Toothpaste
- Plastic wrap
- A plastic spoon
- A marker
- Paper towels

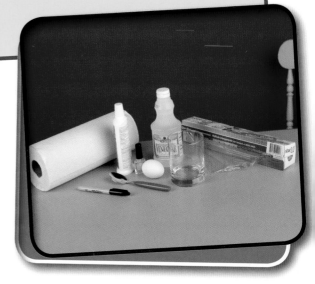

What you do

1 Gently wash the egg in water and dry it with the paper towel.

2 Fill the glass with toothpaste and pat it with a teaspoon to get rid of air bubbles.

3 Draw an "X" on one side of the egg with the marker and cover this mark with nail polish.

4 When the nail polish is dry, put the egg into the toothpaste in the glass, "X" side down, so that the toothpaste covers half the egg. Cover the glass with plastic wrap and leave it at room temperature for four days.

5 Wash the toothpaste off the egg under warm tap water and dry it. Empty the glass and wash it.

6 Put the egg back into the glass and pour in enough vinegar to cover it.

7 Lean the spoon on top of the egg to make sure all of it stays under the vinegar, and cover the glass with plastic wrap. Leave the egg in the vinegar for 8 to 10 hours.

8 Take the egg out of the glass and wash and dry it gently. What has happened?

Conclusion
The acid made the side of the shell not treated with toothpaste soft and weak, but toothpaste has protected the other half of the shell, so it is still hard and strong. This shows how toothpaste protects your teeth if you use it regularly.

Stay safe!
Always wash your hands before and after handling eggs, and only use a small amount of nail polish.

How Do Bacteria Help Us?

Only 1 percent of all known bacteria can make us sick—
the rest are harmless. Many actually help us. In fact, we
wouldn't be able to survive without
bacteria. From the moment
we are born, there are bacteria
in and all over our bodies.

Many kinds of tongue bacteria
fight **infections**, capture skin
cells from the body, and help
break down food.

Some bacteria on our skin
protect us by taking up space
that a more harmful bacterium
would otherwise occupy.

Friendly skin bacteria feed on
the dead skin cells and other
debris on our skin to stop it
from staying on our bodies.

Some bacteria in our **intestine**
help us to digest food.

DID YOU KNOW?

Each square inch of
your skin has about
32 million bacteria
living on it. An adult
has about 4 pounds
(2 kilograms) of
bacteria in the
digestive system—
that is like two full
bags of sugar!

The vast majority of body bacteria live in the digestive system. The useful bacteria in our digestive system help us to break down foods that are hard to **digest** so we can absorb **nutrients** from them. They also destroy bad bacteria, break down harmful substances, and help to develop our **immune system**. The body's immune system recognizes and destroys harmful bacteria, to protect the body from disease.

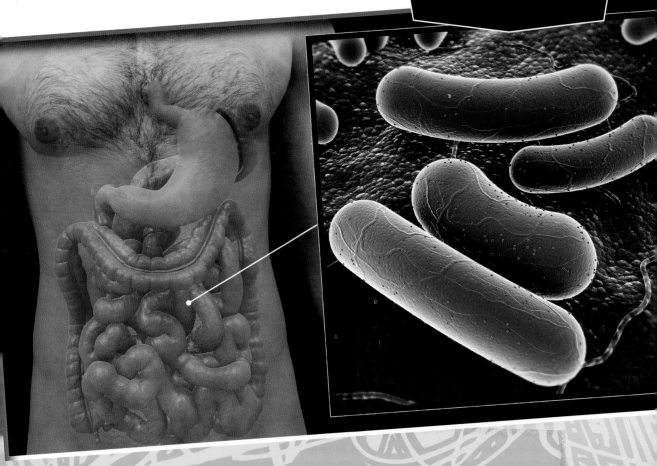

Our intestines are jam-packed with microbes!

Eureka moment!

Scientists have discovered that useful bacteria increase in the stomachs of people who eat high-fiber foods such as onions, bananas, and green vegetables. Bad bacteria like to feed on the sugars and fats found in **processed foods**, so they tend to increase if you eat too many of these foods.

Are there bacteria in yogurt?

We use bacteria to make yogurt and other foods. Yogurt is made by boiling milk and adding *Lactobacillus* bacteria to it. The bacteria feed on the natural sugars in the milk and release lactic acid as waste. This acid makes the milk thicken into yogurt, gives yogurt its tangy taste, and stops any harmful bacteria from growing. Bacteria are also used to make other dairy products, such as cheese and sour cream.

Eureka moment!

In 1908, Elie Metchnikoff won the Nobel Prize for discovering probiotics. These are bacteria found in some foods that people think help us to digest our foods.

Bacteria make the holes in Swiss cheese! Some bacteria make lactic acid and other bacteria eat the acid. They make carbon dioxide gas as waste, which makes bubbles that form the holes.

The process by which microbes break down sugars in foods into other substances is called fermentation. Chocolate is made from cocoa beans that form inside pods on trees. These beans are put into closed boxes. The fruity pulp around the beans ferments with bacteria and other microbes, such as naturally occurring **yeasts**. It is this process that gives the beans their chocolate flavor. People also pickle cucumbers, cabbage, and other vegetables by fermenting them with lactic acid bacteria.

cocoa beans

cocoa pod

DID YOU KNOW?

Soy sauce is thought to be one of the world's oldest food flavorings. It was discovered in China more than 2,500 years ago. It is made naturally by fermenting a mixture of mashed soybeans, wheat, water, and salt.

Without microbes such as bacteria, we wouldn't have delicious bars of chocolate!

Do bacteria help plants grow?

Bacteria help plants to grow. By doing this, they help to provide food for all living things, because animals get nutrients by eating plants or each other. Bacteria that live in soil help to decompose dead plants and animals. As they break down dead remains, they return nutrients from the remains to the soil. Plants use these nutrients to help them grow. Without bacteria in soil, important nutrients would not get recycled and there would be dead plants and animals piled up all around us.

1 Bacteria feed on organic matter in and on soil.

2 They break waste down into tiny pieces of nutrient that wash into the soil.

3 Plants take these nutrients in through their roots to help them grow.

DID YOU KNOW?
A single teaspoon of soil contains more than a billion (1,000,000,000) bacteria!

Microbes recycle waste and provide plants with the nutrients they need.

The nitrogen cycle

Bacteria also provide plants with nitrogen, a gas in the air that all living things need. There is plenty of nitrogen in the air, but plants and animals cannot take it directly from air. That is where bacteria come in. When nitrogen is absorbed by the soil, different bacteria help it to change states so that it can be absorbed by plants. Animals then get their nitrogen from the plants.

Clover, pea, and bean plants have nitrogen-fixing bacteria on their roots, so farmers grow these plants to improve the quality of the soil.

Eureka moment!

In 1888, a German scientist named Hermann Hellriegel explained how certain plants such as peas and beans get nitrogen. They have bacteria living on their roots that convert nitrogen and supply it to the plant. In return, the bacteria receive nutrients they need from the plant.

How Do Bacteria Harm Us?

Bacteria are to blame for all sorts of health problems, from sore throats and ear infections to stomachaches and food poisoning. When pathogens (harmful microorganisms) get inside body cells, they take nutrients and energy from the cells. As the pathogens reproduce, they release harmful substances called toxins. Toxins are poisons that cause things such as runny noses, rashes, coughing, or vomiting (throwing up). They can even damage parts of the body.

Bacteria can spread and get into our bodies in different ways.

Infected people cough or sneeze bacteria into the air and other people breathe them in.

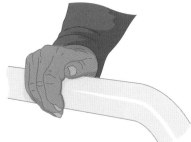

Infected people leave bacteria on things that others touch.

Touching food with dirty hands helps bacteria to spread.

Dirty water contains bacteria.

Many bacteria live on and inside pets and other animals.

Infections

Different bacteria cause different problems. Ear infections happen when a tube between the ear and nose gets blocked (for example, when someone gets a cold). This allows bacteria to build up in the ear, causing pain and fever. *Streptococci* bacteria can cause strep throat and a red rash on the body called scarlet fever. *Salmonella* and *Campylobacter* bacteria can both cause food poisoning. They can occur in raw foods such as eggs and undercooked meat.

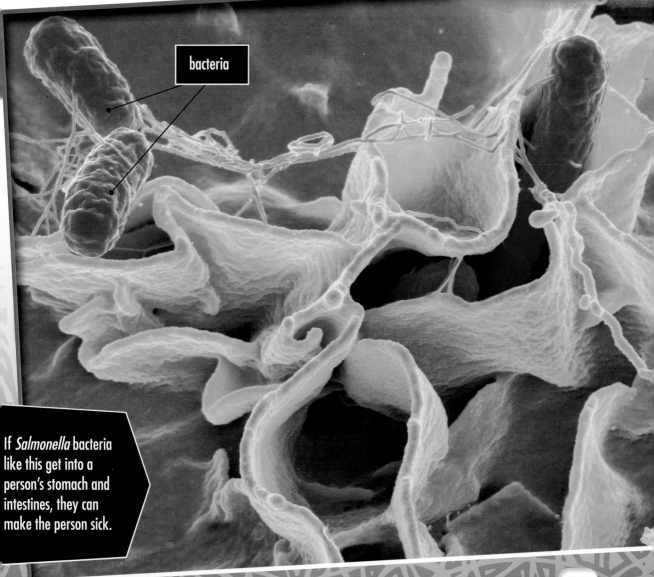

bacteria

If *Salmonella* bacteria like this get into a person's stomach and intestines, they can make the person sick.

What are antibiotics?

When you go to a doctor with a bacterial infection you can't fight off, he or she may give you **antibiotics**. Antibiotics are medicines used to treat infections caused by bacteria. Antibiotics kill harmful bacteria cells or stop them from growing or reproducing. Antibiotics recognize the bacteria cells because they are different than the cells in your body. Some antibiotics can get rid of a range of bacterial infections; others attack particular ones. Antibiotics can work well against bacteria, but they don't work against viruses.

Eureka moment!

Alexander Fleming discovered **penicillin**, the world's first antibiotic, in 1928. Penicillin saved thousands of soldiers' lives in World War II because it killed bacteri that would otherwise ha infected their wounds.

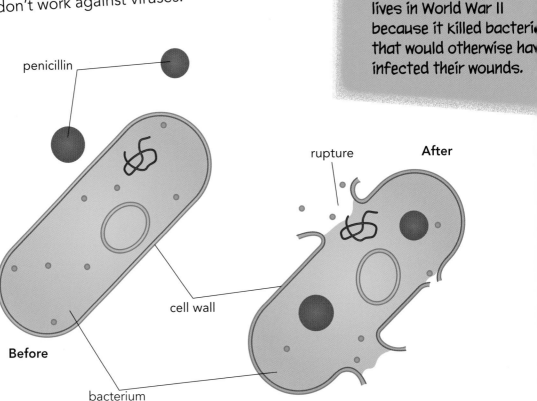

penicillin

rupture

After

cell wall

Before

bacterium

The antibiotic penicillin works by stopping the bacteria from producing a substance that forms the cell wall. This means the cell wall gets weaker and eventually bursts.

If you have an infection, avoid passing it. Only use your own towel, throw away used tissues and bandages, and keep your hands clean.

One problem with antibiotics is that bacteria can become **resistant** to them. This means the bacteria change and antibiotics don't work on them anymore. This happens because some people don't use antibiotics properly. For example, if people don't finish all the antibiotics a doctor gives them, only some of the bacteria are destroyed. The antibiotics may have killed weak bacteria but left some strong bacteria in the body. The more resistant bacteria grow and multiply until antibiotics no longer work on them.

DID YOU KNOW?

Follow these rules to stop bacteria from becoming resistant to antibiotics.

- Only take antibiotics when you need them.
- Always finish a course of antibiotics a doctor gives you.
- Never take out-of-date antibiotics or antibiotics from someone else.
- Never take antibiotics for infections caused by viruses—they won't work!

Try this!

Bacteria and other microbes affect different types of food. Find out why we keep some foods in the refrigerator.

Prediction

Bacteria will grow on food that is not stored in a refrigerator. Different foods will attract different bacteria.

What you need

- Disposable gloves
- Four plates
- One slice of bread
- Half an apple
- One slice of cheese
- One slice of cooked meat
- Water from a faucet
- Sealable plastic sandwich bags
- A magnifying glass

What you do

1 Wearing gloves, put each of the foods out on a clean plate and leave them out at room temperature for 1 hour.

Stay safe!

You should only do this activity with an adult. Don't leave food longer than a week. When you are finished, leave the rotting food in the sealed bags and dispose of them carefully in a garbage can outside.

2 Wearing a new, clean pair of gloves, put each of the foods in a separate plastic bag.

3 Add two tablespoons of water to each bag and then seal the bags tightly. Leave some air in each bag as you close it.

4 Put the sandwich bags in a warm spot, where they can stay undisturbed for a week.

5 Look at each bag every day. Can you see signs of bacteria growing? Use the magnifying glass to help you spot any changes.

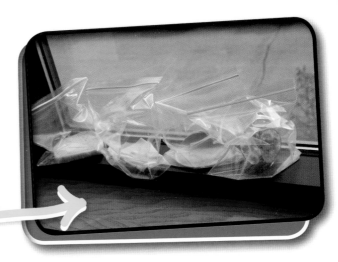

6 Record your results. Which food rots fastest? Describe the changes that you see.

Conclusion

When you left food in the open, bacteria and other microbes got into it. Bacteria grow well in warm, moist places where they have food, so they reproduce quickly in the bags. Bacteria go for some foods, such as meat, more than others. Different types of bacteria may go for different foods, which is why you will see different-colored molds. We put foods in a refrigerator because cool, dry air slows bacteria growth, but even in a refrigerator, food goes bad eventually.

What Are Viruses Like?

There are thousands of different viruses that come in many different shapes, from loops and spiky ovals to thin sticks or bricks with rounded edges. They are found just about everywhere on Earth, including in soil, water, and air. Unlike bacteria, viruses need to be inside another living cell to reproduce. The plant or animal that viruses live inside is called a **host**, and some viruses are so small they can even live inside bacteria!

Eureka moment!

In 1892, a Russian scientist named Dmitri Iwanowski put liquid from diseased tobacco plants through a filter that was designed to trap bacteria. When he injected healthy plants with the filtered liquid, they still got the disease. He was the first person to discover a virus!

Once viruses get inside a host, they reproduce and spread, causing disease, such as plant diseases that ruin crops. The red and white bumps damaging this leaf are caused by a virus.

How viruses spread

Once a virus gets inside a host, it can spread quickly by using the host's own cells to reproduce. First, it either injects part of itself into the cell or the cell swallows it up. Then, the virus takes over the parts of the cell that make the cell work. It uses these to make copies of itself. One virus can make millions of new viruses inside a human cell. Eventually, there are so many copies of the virus that the host's cell bursts. The new viruses spread out and start to take over other cells.

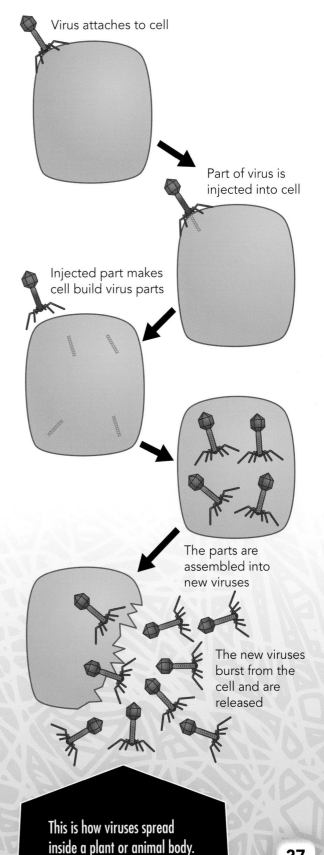

Virus attaches to cell

Part of virus is injected into cell

Injected part makes cell build virus parts

The parts are assembled into new viruses

The new viruses burst from the cell and are released

This is how viruses spread inside a plant or animal body.

DID YOU KNOW?

Viruses do not belong to the five **kingdoms** of life that include animals, plants, bacteria, fungi, and protists. They are smaller and less complex than cells that can reproduce by themselves.

What diseases do viruses cause?

When viruses damage a host's cells, they can cause disease. The most common viral disease is the cold, but viruses can affect all parts of the body. Viruses cause many diseases and can spread quickly from one person to another. Like bacteria, viruses spread by air, water, fluids, touch, and also through animal bites. They can also live for a while outside a host, so they can be passed on via things such as doorknobs.

When people sneeze or cough, droplets from their mouth can carry viruses up to 7 feet (2 meters) away — so sneeze or cough into a tissue!

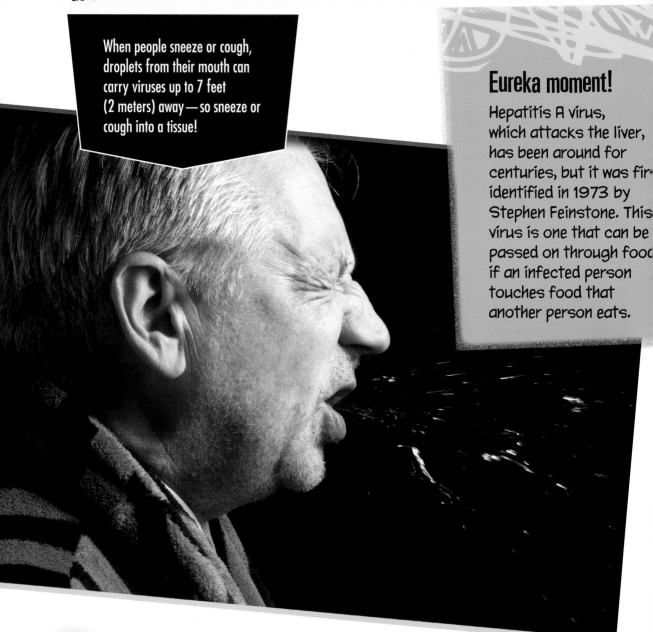

Eureka moment!

Hepatitis A virus, which attacks the liver, has been around for centuries, but it was firs identified in 1973 by Stephen Feinstone. This virus is one that can be passed on through food if an infected person touches food that another person eats.

Fighting viruses

The body's immune system fights off most viruses (and bacteria) that get into the body. If white blood cells in your blood recognize the virus, they make substances called **antibodies** that find and destroy it. These antibodies stay in the blood, ready to destroy similar viruses if they get into the body in the future. Unfortunately, there are too many different cold viruses for this to work with colds.

DID YOU KNOW?

There are over 200 different viruses that can give you a cold. Adults get an average of two colds a year, but children get an average of eight different colds a year, because their immune systems are not as well developed.

Most people only get some viral diseases, such as chickenpox, once. After you have had it, your body recognizes the virus that caused it and is ready to destroy it as soon as it enters your body.

How do we treat viruses?

Scientists have developed medicines for only a few viral diseases, such as severe forms of chickenpox. These stop the virus from multiplying and help people get better more quickly. For less serious viral infections such as colds, people just rest and wait until their immune system cures them. Doctors have also developed vaccines to stop people from catching more serious infections, such as measles. A vaccine contains a dead or harmless form of a virus (or bacteria). When vaccines are injected into the body, the blood makes antibodies that defend people against real viruses in the future.

Some diseases are dangerous and spread rapidly, so doctors give vaccines to large numbers of people at the same time.

WHAT'S NEXT?

It is expensive to train and pay doctors to inject vaccines. In the future, vaccines may be put into foods such as bananas so that people can simply eat them!

Inactive viruses

Sometimes, being infected by a virus doesn't mean you will necessarily get sick. A lot of people have the herpes simplex virus in their body, but most of the time it is inactive. If it becomes active, it causes blisters on the mouth called cold sores. This often happens if the immune system is weakened, such as when you have a cold. That is another reason to keep healthy—so you can fight viruses in your body if they decide to become active.

 DID YOU KNOW?

Viruses can change quickly and can become resistant to vaccines. For example, as soon as a new flu vaccine is made, a new type of flu appears that is different than the last one, and antibodies in your body don't recognize it.

Cold sores clear up after about a week, but you should avoid touching them, sharing towels, or kissing people, as you could pass on the virus.

Where Do Fungi Grow?

Fungi are microorganisms that grow on plants, animals, and dead organic matter. Fungi are neither plants nor animals—they are in a kingdom of their own. Yeasts, molds, and mushrooms all are types of fungi. Yeasts are the only unicellular (single-celled) fungi. You sometimes see them clustered together, forming a white powder on berries. Molds and mushrooms are made of many microscopic cells that grow together, which is why we can see them.

Fungi feed by absorbing nutrients from whatever they are living on. Some fungi are a nuisance and cause diseases in plants and animals. In fact, fungi ruin about a quarter to half of fruit and vegetable crops every year.

Fungi like these molds grow in one place but reproduce by releasing **spores** that blow to new places. You shouldn't eat rotten food like this because it may contain poisonous substances produced by the molds.

Fungal infections

People can get fungal infections, too. They usually grow on skin, nails, or hair. Tinea leaves itchy red rings on the skin. Candida is a yeast that makes skin red, itchy, and swollen—around the nails, for example. Athlete's foot is caused by a type of fungus. It causes swollen toes, cracked skin, itchiness, and a bad smell! Most fungal infections can be treated with antifungal cream.

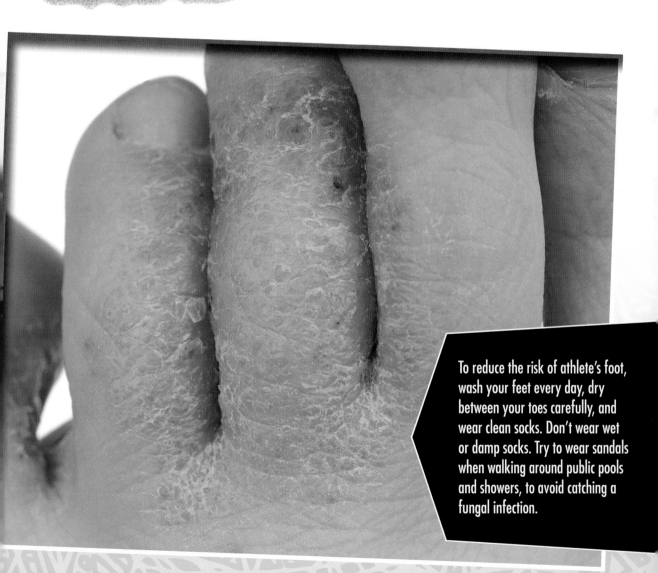

To reduce the risk of athlete's foot, wash your feet every day, dry between your toes carefully, and wear clean socks. Don't wear wet or damp socks. Try to wear sandals when walking around public pools and showers, to avoid catching a fungal infection.

Fungi help us feed. Fun in cows' stomachs help them digest grass, and we eat milk and meat from cattle.

DID YOU KNOW?

Cows and other grass-eating animals have bacteria and also some fungi and **protozoa** in their stomachs. These help them digest tough fibers in grass so they can release sugars to help them to live and grow.

How do we use fungi?

Some fungi are very useful to us. Many mushrooms are safe to eat and provide nutrients we need. We use yeast to make bread. As the yeast ferments, it gives off carbon dioxide gas that gets trapped in the dough and makes the dough rise.

People inject blue cheeses such as Stilton or Roquefort with certain kinds of fungal spores. The mold that grows from these spores gives blue cheeses their color and flavor.

Waste disposal

Fungi also decompose dead plants and animals and keep the world neater. By breaking down organic matter and returning their nutrients to the soil, fungi help plants to grow. These plants provide us with food and other products and raw materials, such as paper and wood. We also use fungi to make some antibiotics. *Penicillium notatum* is the mold from which we get penicillin. Fungi are also used in products that help farmers. Some are used to control nuisance insects, and others are used to control weeds.

Fungi thrive in moist environments such as soil. This is why people wear gloves when gardening and they wash their hands after touching soil.

Try this!

In most of the bread that we eat, yeast is an essential ingredient, mixed with flour and water. What temperature water do you think is best for yeast?

Prediction

Yeast will be most active when mixed with warm water.

What you need

- A balloon pump
- Three balloons
- 1½ packages of active dry yeast
- 1 cup of cold tap water
- 1 cup of warm water
- 1 cup of boiling water
- 12 teaspoons of sugar
- A funnel
- Three small, empty plastic bottles (such as water bottles)

What you do

① Use a balloon pump to blow up and stretch the balloons a few times to make them easier to work with.

② Add half a package of yeast and four teaspoons of sugar to each of the three cups of cold, warm, and boiling water. Stir each cup of water until the yeast and sugar have mixed in with the water.

③ Use the funnel to help you to pour the water mixtures into the bottles.

4 Put the opening of a balloon over the mouth of each bottle. Pull the stem part of the balloons down so that they won't come off easily. Then put all three bottles in the same, safe place where you can watch them.

5 You should notice a change after about 15 minutes. Draw or make a chart with your results.

Conclusion

Yeast is alive but inactive. Warm water makes it active. As the warm, active yeast feeds on sugar, it releases carbon dioxide gas that slowly fills up the balloon. Very cold or boiling water can keep yeast inactive or kill it, which is why those balloons don't blow up.

Stay safe!

Ask an adult to help you with this activity, since it needs boiling water, which can scald you. You might also need some help getting the mouth of the balloons over the top of the bottles. Ask the adult to dispose of the yeast mixture carefully.

What Are Protists?

Most protists are unicellular microorganisms. There are three main types: protozoa, algae, and slime molds. They live in ponds, lakes, seas, and other waters. Many types of protozoa help us. For example, **sewage** treatment plants use some protozoa to help digest raw sewage so that it can be released safely into the sea. Amoebas are helpful protozoa that eat some of the algae that can spread and clog up ponds, lakes, and streams. Dinoflagellates live mostly in the sea and many make their food by photosynthesis, so they are an important part of ocean **food chains**.

DID YOU KNOW?

In darkness, some dinoflagellates give off bright blue light in response to movement within the water. They use it to scare off animals that hunt them.

When dinoflagellates glow in the dark like this, it is called bioluminescence.

Problem protists

Some protists cause illness because they live inside other organisms and take food from them. Some protist molds attack food such as potatoes and corn, destroying whole crops. Amoebas living in dirty water give people dysentery that causes severe diarrhea. Protists get into human bodies by touch or through insect bites, or when people walk barefoot in dirty water or soil, drink dirty water, or eat unwashed raw food.

Malaria is a disease caused by *Plasmodium* protozoa. Mosquitoes carry them and pass them to humans when they bite. Malaria kills around one million people a year.

Eureka moment!

Sleeping sickness is a deadly disease that can cause such a deep sleep that people die. In 1903, Scottish scientist David Bruce proved that insects could carry dangerous protozoa and showed that the protozoan responsible for sleeping sickness was passed on in tsetse fly bites.

Are algae useful?

Some algae are very useful. Microscopic algae are found in fresh and salt water and on damp rocks, trees, and soil. They make their own food by photosynthesis, so other organisms in these habitats either eat them or become food for other organisms that eat them. Microscopic algae also produce a large amount of the oxygen animals breathe, by the process of photosynthesis.

 DID YOU KNOW?

Diatoms are unicellular algae with cell walls made from silica, a kind of natural glass. Dead diatoms sink to the seabed. People collect their glass-like shells to make powders for products such as toothpaste.

Algae can help animals, too! Sloths look green because microscopic algae grow on their damp fur. In return for giving algae a home, the sloth gets a green camouflage color that disguises it as it moves slowly around trees.

Nuisance algae

Some algae are a nuisance. When **fertilizers** and other chemicals wash off land into ponds, lakes, and streams, algae feed on the nutrients and quickly spread. Soon algae cover the water's surface, blocking sunlight that underwater plants need to grow. When the algae die, bacteria break them down. As they do so, they destroy the oxygen that living things in water need to survive. Some algae release poisonous substances into water that build up in fish that people then eat, causing diseases that can be fatal.

WHAT'S NEXT?

Some scientists suggest that we put nutrients into the ocean to increase algae there. Carbon dioxide contributes to **global warming**. Lots of algae could absorb some of the carbon dioxide from the air. When the algae died and sank to the ocean floor, they would take the carbon dioxide with them.

When algae spread over an area of water, it is called an algal bloom.

How Can We Stay Safe with Microbes?

Most microorganisms are safe and some harmful ones are speedily destroyed by the body, but there are some precautions we can all take to reduce the risk of pathogens getting into our bodies.

- Wash your hands well before and after touching any food, after using the bathroom, after touching animals or animal waste, after coughing, sneezing, or blowing your nose, and after visiting sick people.
- Cover your mouth when you cough or sneeze.
- Keep away from other people if you have an illness that is easily spread, to stop the germs from spreading.

Everyone thinks they know how to wash their hands, but few do it properly!

1 Wet your hands with clean water (warm or cold) straight from a faucet. Add soap and rub your hands together to make a lather.

2 Rub the backs of your hands, between your fingers, and under your nails. Rub for at least 20 seconds.

3 Rinse your hands under running water.

4 Dry your hands using a clean towel or let them dry in the air.

Safety steps

Every year, millions of people get sick from pathogens passed on in foods, but most of these illnesses are preventable if we handle food safely.

1 Keep clean! Use clean hands, equipment, and work surfaces and keep pets and insects away from food.
2 Keep raw meat, poultry, and seafood away from other foods and use separate equipment to prepare them. Raw foods can contain dangerous microorganisms that can pass into other foods in the kitchen.
3 Cook and reheat food thoroughly at over 158 degrees Fahrenheit (70 degrees Celsius), especially meat, poultry, eggs, and seafood, as this kills most pathogens.
4 Keep food at safe temperatures. Try to keep hot food hot and don't leave it out at room temperature for more than two hours. Keep cooked and cooled food, and any other food that may go bad, in the refrigerator, preferably below 41 degrees Fahrenheit (5 degrees Celsius).

Make sure you enjoy eating your food, and don't give microorganisms a fighting chance!

Glossary

acid substance that can burn or damage things it touches

antibiotic medicine that treats infections caused by bacteria

antibody substance that the body produces in the blood to fight disease

atmosphere layer of gases that surround Earth

carbon dioxide gas in the air, also known as CO_2

cell smallest unit of a living thing that can exist on its own, carrying out a range of life processes. Most organisms are made of many cells.

cell wall outer covering of a cell

decompose rot or break something down into smaller and smaller pieces until it disappears

digest break down food so that an animal can get the nutrients it needs from the food

evolve when a type of plant or animal slowly changes over many generations and a long period of time

fertilizer substance people put on plants to help them grow bigger and produce more fruit or flowers

flagellum (plural: **flagella**) hair-like part that microorganisms use for movement

food chain sequence of living things that are eaten or eat each other in a particular habitat—for example, a forest

global warming increase in the temperature of Earth's atmosphere, probably caused by the burning of fossil fuels such as coal and oil

host animal or plant on which another animal or plant lives and feeds

immune system system in your body that produces substances to help it fight infections and diseases

inactive not working or feeding; taking a long rest

infection illness that is caused by microorganisms such as bacteria or viruses

intestine long tube in the digestive system connecting the stomach and bottom

kingdom one of the five groups that scientists usually divide living things into: plants, animals, bacteria, fungi, and protists

microbe another word for *microorganism*

microscope device that produces enlarged images of objects that are normally too small to see

nutrient variety of chemicals found in food that animals need to be healthy

organic of or from living things

oxygen type of gas in the air that we need to breathe

pathogen microorganism that can cause infections

penicillin antibiotic used to prevent bacteria from multiplying, as in infected wounds. It got its name because it was first made from the *Penicillin notatum* fungi.

photosynthesis process in green plants that uses the Sun's energy to make glucose from carbon dioxide and water

processed food convenience food that has been cooked and prepared in a factory

protozoan or **protozoon** (plural: **protozoa** or **protozoans**) single-celled animal such as an amoeba

reproduction when a living thing makes offspring like itself

resistant when a microorganism is resistant to a medicine, it means the medicine won't work on it

sewage waste water from bathrooms

spore part that some living things release and use to reproduce

unicellular made up of a single cell

yeast single-celled fungi

Find Out More

Books

Biskup, Agnieszka. *Vampires and Cells* (Monster Science). Mankato, Minn.: Capstone, 2012.

Rooney, Anne. *Infectious Diseases* (Mapping Global Issues). Mankato, Minn.: Smart Apple Media, 2012.

Spilsbury, Richard. *Body Invaders* (Zoom in On). Berkeley Heights, N.J.: Enslow, 2013.

Weakland, Mark. *Gut Bugs, Dust Mites, and Other Microorganisms You Can't Live Without* (Fact Finders). Mankato, Minn.: Capstone, 2011.

Winston, Robert. *Life As We Know It.* New York: Dorling Kindersley, 2012.

Web sites

www.biology4kids.com/files/micro_main.html

Learn more about microorganisms on this web site.

www.kidsbiology.com/biology_basics

Visit this site to explore more about living things, kingdoms, viruses, and more.

kidshealth.org/kid/talk/qa/germs.html

Find out more about "germs" at this KidsHealth site.

Place to visit

The Health Museum
1515 Hermann Drive
Houston, Texas 77004

www.mhms.org

At this museum, you can discover more about you, your body, and what causes illness and other health problems.

Further research

- Find out more about the various ways scientists are trying to use bacteria to produce fuels and to get rid of waste safely.

- Why not find out more about the common cold? We all get colds, but do you know why we get hot when we have a cold? Or why we get them more often in winter?

- You could also discover more about how life on Earth developed after it began with bacteria, and how bacteria and protists contributed to the development of the other kingdoms of life.

Index